for the
LOVE
of
LIBRARIES

A BOOK OF POSTCARDS

PHOTOGRAPHS AND ANECDOTES BY DIANE ASSÉO GRILICHES

INTRODUCTION BY JOHN Y. COLE, DIRECTOR, THE CENTER FOR THE BOOK
IN THE LIBRARY OF CONGRESS

Pomegranate

SAN FRANCISCO

Pomegranate
Box 6099
Rohnert Park, CA 94927

Pomegranate Europe Ltd.
Fullbridge House, Fullbridge
Maldon, Essex CM9 4LE
England

ISBN 0-7649-0609-7
Pomegranate Catalog No. A927

Pomegranate publishes books of postcards on a wide range of subjects. Please write to the
publisher for more information.

Designed by Shannon Lemme
Printed in Korea

07 06 05 04 03 02 01 00   10 9 8 7 6 5 4

To facilitate detachment of the postcards from this book, fold each card along its perforation line before tearing.

"*O*f course you can. Just wander around and look at the books," the librarian behind the desk told the timid thirteen-year-old in the Carnegie Library in Ellensburg, a small town in the middle of Washington State. "This is unbelievable," I remember thinking as I quickly scurried into the adult fiction room before she could change her mind. Opportunity! And I was hooked—on libraries and on reading.

Here are two of the best things about libraries: they are everywhere (the American Library Association counts more than 100,000 in the United States), and they are constantly changing. On-line services, the Internet, and CD-ROMs are part of today's library world, as are videos, recordings, and works of art that can be borrowed. Yet, as this compelling collection of photographs by Diane Asséo Griliches makes clear, somehow there is nothing quite as poignant—or as meaningful—as the magical combination of library, book, and individual reader. In my case—and perhaps for you, too—her photographs also invariably bring back the memory of "my first public library."

The Center for the Book in the Library of Congress was one of the sponsors of Diane Asséo Griliches's book *Library: The Drama Within*, published in 1996 in association with the University of New Mexico Press. The center also was pleased to host an exhibition of Griliches's photographs, many of which appear in this book of postcards, at the Library of Congress early in 1997. This partnership is a natural one, for Griliches's work evokes and embodies the center's purpose: to stimulate public interest in books, reading, and libraries. Today, the center's national reading promotion network includes thirty-four affiliated state centers and more than fifty national education and civic organizations. In addition to their own reading-related activities, these organizations are helping the Center for the Book promote "Building a Nation of Readers," our theme and the basis for activities for the years 1997–2000.

Libraries and the readers who inhabit and draw from them are a dynamic and resilient alliance, an alliance that enriches the present and prepares a better future—an alliance whose practical and emotional appeal is beautifully evoked in these remarkable photographs.

John Y. Cole
Director
The Center for the Book
in the Library of Congress

FOR THE LOVE OF LIBRARIES

WIDENER LIBRARY, Harvard University,
Cambridge, Massachusetts

. . . the studious silence of the library . . . Tranquil brightness.
—James Joyce

A poster of Berenice Abbott's photograph of James Joyce
is inside an office door, illuminated by daylight from the
office windows. The Widener houses the Harvard College
Library and is the largest university library in the world.

Pomegranate   Box 6099   Rohnert Park, CA 94927

FOR THE LOVE OF LIBRARIES

WILLIAM RAINEY HARPER MEMORIAL LIBRARY,
NORTH READING ROOM, UNIVERSITY OF CHICAGO, ILLINOIS

The beautiful large Gothic campus of the University of
Chicago was built in the 1890s on a flat and treeless plain,
creating its own landscape there. Gargoyles hover on the
edges as shadows from the Gothic arches play on the
modern lounges. William Rainey Harper was the
university's first president.

POMEGRANATE BOX 6099 ROHNERT PARK CA 94927

FOR THE LOVE OF LIBRARIES

KOBE UNIVERSITY LIBRARY, KOBE, JAPAN

An afternoon nap, while not exactly condoned, is at least
tolerated in the spirit of humanitarian laissez-faire.

—Bruce A. Shuman

The university library survived the devastating earthquake
in Kobe, although thirty-nine students lost their lives.

POMEGRANATE BOX 6099 ROHNERT PARK CA 94927

For the Love of Libraries

REDWOOD LIBRARY AND ATHENAEUM,
NEWPORT, RHODE ISLAND

This is the oldest circulating library in the country that still operates in its original location. It was built in 1748 by Peter Harrison, the architect of Newport's Touro Synagogue, the oldest surviving synagogue in America. Readers may sit in a cozy corner, surrounded by an important collection of portrait paintings, busts, eighteenth-century furniture, and a book collection with major strengths in the arts and humanities, most of which circulates.

POMEGRANATE   BOX 6099   ROHNERT PARK CA 94927

FOR THE LOVE OF LIBRARIES

NEWTON FREE LIBRARY, NEWTON, MASSACHUSETTS

Read meanwhile . . . Hunt among the shelves, as dogs do grasses . . .
                                            —Randall Jarrell

POMEGRANATE   BOX 6099   ROHNERT PARK, CA 94927

FOR THE LOVE OF LIBRARIES

MASSACHUSETTS CORRECTIONAL INSTITUTION
LAW LIBRARY, NORFOLK, MASSACHUSETTS

*Ten guards and the warden couldn't have torn me out of those books.
Months passed without even thinking about being imprisoned. . . . I
had never been so truly free in my life.* —Malcolm X

This library is in the medium security prison where Malcolm X
was held. He was transferred to Norfolk on the request of his
sister, since the library and the educational-rehabilitation
program are its outstanding features.

POMEGRANATE   BOX 6099   ROHNERT PARK, CA 94927

FOR THE LOVE OF LIBRARIES

NEW YORK PUBLIC LIBRARY, Reading Room 315, New York City

Despite the comings and goings of the patrons, the atmosphere of this monumental Reading Room is one of quiet intensity. This commodious space has nurtured generations of writers and scholars, and given comfort and knowledge to many an ordinary citizen.

POMEGRANATE   BOX 6099   ROHNERT PARK, CA 94927

FOR THE LOVE OF LIBRARIES

PERKINS SCHOOL FOR THE BLIND LIBRARY,
WATERTOWN, MASSACHUSETTS

The book markers give the Braille library a unique appearance. The Perkins also has a tremendous selection of unabridged books on tape from the Library of Congress, which it mails to the blind, free of charge.

As long as I can read, nothing human is beyond my understanding, nothing is totally foreign to my nature . . . there are no limits to my being . . . I'm never alone.   —Linda Weltner

POMEGRANATE BOX 6099 ROHNERT PARK CA 94927

FOR THE LOVE OF LIBRARIES

THE LIBRARY OF CONGRESS, Main Reading Room, Washington, D.C.

This view from Shakespeare's foot looks down from under a 160-foot-high dome. With its 110 million items, which include approximately 20 million books, the Library of Congress is the most comprehensive collection of knowledge in the world. Each day, 31,000 new items come into its mailroom. Its twenty-one reading rooms are open to the public.

Pomegranate Box 6099 Rohnert Park CA 94927

For the Love of Libraries

NOXUBEE COUNTY LIBRARY, Macon, Mississippi

This library was originally built as a jail in 1907. When the old jail was closed, the citizens of Macon raised funds to convert it into a library, and they preserved its unique "decor." So, along with the barred cells, a rope hook and trap door for the gallows were left on the third floor.

Why is there not a Majesty's library in every county town? There is a Majesty's gaol in every one. —Thomas Carlyle

Pomegranate Box 6099 Rohnert Park CA 94927

FOR THE LOVE OF LIBRARIES

THE FOLGER SHAKESPEARE LIBRARY,
WASHINGTON, D.C.

Come, take choice of all my library, and so beguile thy sorrow.
—William Shakespeare

The world's largest collection of Shakespeareana resides at the Folger Shakespeare Library. Henry Clay Folger and his wife, Emily Jordan Folger, had a passion for Shakespeare and spent a lifetime collecting these treasures. When they decided to give them to the American public, Congress voted to build the Folger Library as a major research center.

POMEGRANATE   BOX 6099   ROHNERT PARK CA 94927

FOR THE LOVE OF LIBRARIES

EMMA YATES MEMORIAL LIBRARY,
POCAHONTAS, VIRGINIA

*A library is books and somewhere to put them and some people
to want them there . . .*   —Sheila Bourbeau

When Emma Yates died, the family turned over her hat
store to the people of this small coal-mining town to
convert to a library of donated books, run by two
volunteer librarians.

POMEGRANATE   BOX 6099   ROHNERT PARK CA 94927

FOR THE LOVE OF LIBRARIES

TULKARM PUBLIC MUNICIPAL LIBRARY,
TULKARM, PALESTINE

In the library, I discovered that you could learn by following your nose. And I learned that a book was as close to a living thing as you could get without being one. —Bill Harley

POMEGRANATE BOX 6099 ROHNERT PARK CA 94927

FOR THE LOVE OF LIBRARIES

BOSTON PUBLIC LIBRARY, Newspaper Room,
Boston, Massachusetts

Among patrons needing current or back issues of
newspapers are those (usually men) who make a ritual of
coming in to read the daily papers.

Pomegranate   Box 6099   Rohnert Park CA 94927

FOR THE LOVE OF LIBRARIES

PIERPONT MORGAN LIBRARY, New York City

This boy was on a class trip from Brooklyn to the Morgan
Library. The library, an Italianate palazzo designed by Charles
Follen McKim, was built in 1906 by the financier and
voracious collector of literature and art J. Pierpont Morgan.
In 1924 the library was made public by Morgan's son, who felt
that its holdings were too important to keep private.

POMEGRANATE   BOX 6099   ROHNERT PARK CA 94927

FOR THE LOVE OF LIBRARIES

BIBLIOTEKA IVAN PAŠTRIĆ, SPLIT, CROATIA

*We had that peculiar thrill which comes from going into a room
redolent with the faint mustiness of old calf and feeling that
almost any volume may turn out a treasure.* —Harold J. Laski

The Communists closed the seminary that housed this
library but allowed the seminarians to keep the library in
two small, windowless rooms.

POMEGRANATE   BOX 6099   ROHNERT PARK, CA 94927

FOR THE LOVE OF LIBRARIES

HUNGARIAN LIBRARY, Jerusalem, Israel

This library is squeezed into three tiny, cluttered rooms off a small street in downtown Jerusalem. The librarian said it's difficult for Hungarian immigrants to learn Hebrew, and the old people often take out books in Hungarian that they had read in their childhood. "Perhaps they are looking for their youth," she said.

Pomegranate   Box 6099   Rohnert Park, CA 94927

BENJAMIN FRANKLIN
1706–1790
Attributed to sculptor
OWEN WOOD
FRANK WOOD

FOR THE LOVE OF LIBRARIES

BOSTON PUBLIC LIBRARY, Bates Reading Room,
Boston, Massachusetts

*He grew dutifully, conspicuously studious, spending long
afternoons in the town library, watched over by a white plaster
bust of Ben Franklin.* —David McCullough Truman

Pomegranate Box 6099 Rohnert Park CA 94927

FOR THE LOVE OF LIBRARIES

THE LONDON LIBRARY, London, England

This is the largest independent lending library in the world, a "private" library of five or six thousand readers. Members (anyone may join for a reasonable fee) have access to the stacks and may borrow almost any book it owns, including old and rare ones. It was founded in 1841 by Thomas Carlyle, who was fed up with existing library facilities in London. Dickens was one of its founding members, Tennyson an early president, and T. S. Eliot its president in the 1960s.

Pomegranate Box 6099 Rohnert Park CA 94927

FOR THE LOVE OF LIBRARIES

CALOUSTE GULBENKIAN LIBRARY OF THE
ARMENIAN PATRIARCHATE, JERUSALEM, ISRAEL

This library is in the Armenian quarter of the Old City of
Jerusalem. It was established in 1929 by Calouste
Gulbenkian, a famous Armenian philanthropist, and since
then it has received thousands of books from Armenia,
Lebanon, Egypt, and the Armenian diaspora in the United
States. One-third of the library's materials are in
Armenian. The library is open for research, but it has also
served as the cultural and educational center for the
Armenians in Israel.

POMEGRANATE BOX 6099 ROHNERT PARK CA 94927

FOR THE LOVE OF LIBRARIES

CAMBRIDGE PUBLIC LIBRARY,
CAMBRIDGE, MASSACHUSETTS

When I got my library card, that's when my life began.
—Rita Mae Brown

POMEGRANATE   BOX 6099   ROHNERT PARK, CA 94927

FOR THE LOVE OF LIBRARIES

BIBLIOTECA MARUCELLIANA, FLORENCE, ITALY

The student has his Rome, his Florence, his whole glowing Italy,
within the four walls of his library. He has in his books the
ruins of an antique world, and the glories of a modern one.
—Henry Wadsworth Longfellow

POMEGRANATE   BOX 6099   ROHNERT PARK, CA 94927

FOR THE LOVE OF LIBRARIES

BIBLIOTHÈQUE SAINTE-GENEVIÈVE,
PARIS, FRANCE

*When I step into this library, I cannot understand why I ever
step out of it.* — Marie de Sévigné

There is a poetic quality to this space in the early morning
before it opens to the rush of university students. In the
Middle Ages, the library was housed in the Abbey of
Sainte-Geneviève. The present edifice was built by Henri
Labrouste and is a reflection of the new industrial age,
with its iron frame and wrought-iron decorations.

POMEGRANATE BOX 6099 ROHNERT PARK CA 94927

FOR THE LOVE OF LIBRARIES

CLEVELAND DEPOT LITERACY LIBRARY,
CLEVELAND, MISSISSIPPI

Built in 1884, the railroad ran from New Orleans up to
Memphis, and new towns like Cleveland, Mississippi, were
created along the route. President Grover Cleveland, after
whom the town was named, William Jennings Bryan, and
President Theodore Roosevelt made whistle stops here.
The train stopped running in the 1960s. The abandoned
depot was recently converted to a special Library for
Adult Literacy and has three hundred students.

POMEGRANATE BOX 6099 ROHNERT PARK CA 94927

FOR THE LOVE OF LIBRARIES
THOMAS CRANE PUBLIC LIBRARY,
QUINCY, MASSACHUSETTS

Libraries . . . those temples of learning, those granite-and-marble monuments . . .

—Susan Allen Toth

POMEGRANATE   BOX 6099   ROHNERT PARK, CA 94927

FOR THE LOVE OF LIBRARIES

SHREWSBURY BOOKMOBILE,
SHREWSBURY, MASSACHUSETTS

*When I . . . discovered libraries, it was like having Christmas
every day!* —Jean Fritz

As the library bus rounded the corner and assumed its
usual place, children and adults poured out into the street.
It was as attractive as an ice cream wagon.

POMEGRANATE   BOX 6099   ROHNERT PARK, CA 94927

FOR THE LOVE OF LIBRARIES

LOS ANGELES CENTRAL LIBRARY,
Los Angeles, California

*To my thinking, a great librarian must have a clear head, a
strong hand, and above all, a great heart . . . and I am inclined
to think that most of the men who will achieve this greatness
will be women.* —Melvil Dewey

Pomegranate Box 6099 Rohnert Park CA 94927

FOR THE LOVE OF LIBRARIES

BIBLIOTHÈQUE NATIONALE, PARIS, FRANCE

I have always imagined that Paradise will be a kind of library.
—Jorge Luis Borges

This glorious reading room was built in 1862 by Henri Labrouste, who also built the Bibliothèque Sainte-Geneviève, and has nine domes, each with an "eye" providing natural light from above. The roof is supported with twelve slender iron columns.

POMEGRANATE   BOX 6099   ROHNERT PARK CA 94927

FOR THE LOVE OF LIBRARIES

CAMBRIDGE PUBLIC LIBRARY,
CENTRAL SQUARE BRANCH, CAMBRIDGE, MASSACHUSETTS

These kids had entered into the world of the story.
Neither the librarian turning pages nor the presence of a
photographer could bring them out of it.

POMEGRANATE BOX 6099 ROHNERT PARK CA 94927

FOR THE LOVE OF LIBRARIES

WIDENER LIBRARY, Harvard University,
Cambridge, Massachusetts

*They kiss in cubicles; for all we know they breed down there in the
twelfth century.* —Larry Rubin

Pomegranate   Box 6099   Rohnert Park CA 94927

POMEGRANATE BOOKS OF POSTCARDS
ON PHOTOGRAPHY, HISTORY, AND RELATED SUBJECTS

Pomegranate publishes books of postcards on a wide range of subjects.
Please write to the publisher for more information.

Massachusetts Correctional Institution Law Library, Norfolk, Massachusetts

ibraries perhaps have never been more precious to us than they are today, as many of th peril due to cutbacks in funds and what can seem to be a dwindling understanding importance in our lives. This collection of dramatic, inviting, even romantic photographs b Asséo Griliches emphatically declares that the worth and benefits of libraries—stalwart havens of cu centuries—cannot be underestimated or taken for granted and should never be denied. Indee photographs attest to the fact that libraries are some of the most sacred places we can ever hope

Pomegranate

CONTAINS THIRTY OVERSIZED POSTCARDS

$9.95 (14.95 CAN.)A927   ISBN 0-7649-

7 17194 00927 5   9 780764 90

CAT PLACES

PHOTOGRAPHS BY
FRED GESCHEIDT

A BOOK OF POSTCARDS